E HOLLEY

PAUL RIEGE MY GRANDMOTHER HELEN MCCABE

MY GREAT-GRANDMOTHER NELLIE NATONAB

GRACE MY GREAT-GRANDMOTHER NELLIE NATONAB

POLY STYRENE JAUNE QUICK-TO-SEE-SMITH

RED EARTH TONES

OCHRE

DIONNE BRAND TINA CAMPT

SAIDIYA HARTMAN JENN AN

TONI MORRISON

CARRIE MAE WEEMS

ZORA NEAL HURSTON SADE

MARY LOU WILLIAMS

BLACK BLUE

WESTIN TERUYA

ADEE ROBERSON LEILA MAYSOUN WAZWAZ

MICHELE CARLSON

ESSENCE HARDEN

PURPLE ANYTHIN
DARK

IDIGO BLUE

G000080535

MAXINE HONG KINGSTON

LENY STROBEL

PINK

FU

MELINDA

EVELINA GALANG

VIRGINA CERENIO

JANICE SAPIGO

TRINIDAD ES

CELIA H. RODRIGUEZ

DR. DAWN MA

CHERRIE MORAGA

TA BAKER

GLORIA ANZALDUA

GOLD

CHERRIE MORAGA

FRANK LA PINA

CRAFT: EMBROIDERY, THREAD

WEAVING, GLYPHS, PETRO

CELIA

PICTOGRAMS, STORY, STO

JOSE MONTOYA

GLORIA AN

ESTEBAN VILLA

NATURE

FAIRY TALES

WINNIE MANDELA

S

I YANIF

ANA CAST

G

KORRYN GAINES

SAN

IDDEAL

GREEN

GLORIA ANZALDUA

SARAH LAWRENCE LIGHTFOOT

ANGELA DAVIS

BLAC

RED MAYA DOLORES HUERTA

BELL HOOKS

MAMA HELENA VIRAMONTES

MAYA ANGELOU DONA CHAVEZ

MY GRANDMOTHER

BLACK

PURPLE TON

LAVENDER

BABY
BLUE ANISIKA NAZAK

BELL HOOKS BEIG

ALICE WALKER SHAH

AH ZORA NEAL HURSTON

ISAH TEISH AUDRE LORDE

CELIA

JAQUI ALEXANDER GOLDEN
YELLOW

BLAND PURPLE

GINE FOREST GREEN

PUSHPAMALA N

ABI JUANITA

K SHAHMUSH PARSIPUA

V. ANCESTOR CAMILA NALINI M

ROBIN BERNSTEIN GLORIA ANZALDUA

VANIA MICHELINI-CASTILLO

CK LADZEKPO HOPE GINSBURG

LUIS BARRAGAN ARATA ISOZAKI

ALLAN DESOUZA TURQU

B DUBOVSKY & CHICVEYI COATL PASTOR VEGA

THERESA HAK KYUM CHA

MINERVA CUEVAS DAUGHTERS

TANIA BRUGUERA N

FRANCIS ALYS ESTELA ROMAN SA

E REGINA JOSÉ GALINDO ALL SIS

WILLIAM POPE L.

SHIRIN NESHAT PUR

PATRISIA GONZALES

TEH CHING HSIEH EDGAR CAYCE

CRUZ GUILLERMO GOMEZ PEÑA

ISABEL ALLENDE BUENA VISTA SOCIAL CLUB

MICHAEL JACKSON ERYKAH BADU DAN

CHAVELA VARGAS MALA RODRIGUEZ

MARE AD

QUINCY JONES BEING A PART
OF STANDING ROCK

RED CLAY

BEESWAX YELLOW

RED

I

PURPLE

E

ONYINYE

ANA MENDIETA
NATALIE MBIKABA
   ALMA BLACKWELL
ESTHER GOOLSBY
     MISS TOWANDA SHERRY
H.P. BLAVATSKY

GOLD

JÖRN KARLSSON

M

   KUDZAY CHIMALKA

AHMED

   WOMYN

OTHERS

BLACK

RED

PRUSSIAN BLUE

WILLIAMS

TENKA LIRIKA

XICAN PINK

Cover
"Eyes (Relational)" 30" x 22.25", Xerox lithograph on paper
Grace Rosario Perkins, 2017

Inside Cover
"Our roots have so much overlap," Pen, colored pencil
Lukaza Branfman-Verissimo, 2018

Plant Illustrations
"Medicinas," Pencil, paper.
Vreni Michelini Castillo, 2018

Design
Justin Carder

WOLFMAN BOOKS

410 13th St. Oakland, CA 94612
wolfmanhomerepair.com

Distributed by
Small Press Distribution
spdbooks.org

978-0-9983461-7-5

2019 • Printed in Canada

COLOR

THEORY

For our grandmothers who held us with their own two hands and remind us that love and liberation are present when we speak our truth.

Para nuestras abuelitas que nos apapacharon y nos recuerdan que el amor y nuestra libertad se manifiestan cuando honramos nuestra verdad.

Contents

Introduction

Introduction

"Que hacen las hormigas?"
—Celia Herrera Rodríguez

We are a circle, our center is everywhere, expanding; we hold the circumference.

We are the backbone: the ants—carrying, making new paths, aerating, working collectively, keeping the disregarded, preserving and persisting.

We strategize together to protect one another and care for the land—labor learned through the hands of our ancestors.

We work within, inside / outside of the art world, recovering, rebuilding and revitalizing.

We are nomadic: growing in the outskirts, outside of the metropolitan area, in basements and gardens, within the intercity, in offices and museums, in schools and forests.

We queer cultural and political boundaries—it is here where we restore freedom.

We are not afraid of color, because we are the embodiment of color.

We come together in this book, reflecting on the past, calling out the present and reimagining the future.

—Maya Gomez & Vreni Michelini Castillo

Restore memory. Let the one who is *diseuse*, one who is daughter restore spring with her each appearance from beneath the earth. The ink spills thickest before it runs dry before it stops writing at all.

—Theresa
Hak Kyung Cha

If colour is unimportant, I began to wonder, why is it so important to exclude it so forcefully? If colour doesn't matter, why does its abolition matter so much?

—David Batchelor

Yoga Negra

Onyinye Alheri

Welcome to Yoga Negra,
a guided meditation practice.
Please lie down in a comfortable position;
here on my back should do.
Place a blanket over your body;
the darker the better
to not be seen.
Make sure you are warm and comfortable.
And if you can not
I will.
Spread your legs.
Spread your arms, palms up.
There's no escape for you anyway.
In silence,
bring your awareness to any cracks of the bone
or groans that come forth
as you gently distribute your weight upon my
I mean your
spine.
Please resist the temptation to speak during the
practice of yoga negra.
I assure you, you will be
silenced,
doubted,
corrected.

Inhale and receive the pleasure I create for you.
Exhale and release your pain unto me.
Inhale.
Exhale.
Inhale.
Exhale.
Cultivate sensations of lightness in all of your parts.
Cultivate an awareness of your spirit residing in this plane.
Let the body become heavy as you sink into the dirt.
Head.
Neck.
Shoulders.
Arms.
Torso.
Legs.
Feet.
Awaken the knowing of deep heaviness in your heart.
Notice the sounds around you:
The multitude of *no's* and *not enough's* that bounce from left brain to right.
Bring your awareness to the hurt parts of you
If you find that hurt resides in a multitude of places,
Let your consciousness dance from one axis to an-

other:
Left eye.
Right thigh.
Buttocks.
Inner heart.
Vulva.
Liver.
Lower lip, busted?
Upper ribs, cracked?
Left leg, hip to knee
Right leg, hip to knee
Swollen soles
Arteries.
Nipples.
Deltoids.
Palm of hand, both left and right.
Bring your attention to my voice.
Feel me receiving this heaviness.
Remain with the awareness of residing in this co-
coon.
A buffer to your pain,
a vessel of your pleasure.
Bring your awareness to my line curves,
waves,
edges,

deep tones
of voice and flesh,
boundless soul,
and steel will.
All best taken softened

and bleached.
Diluted in at least 8 ounces of fluid,
any of my humours will do.
Take your pick:
Bile, phlegm, or blood.
When you have finished drinking of my rivers,
lick your lips.
Savor it.
Gently wiggle your toes and fingers.
Point your arms and legs in a loooong stretch.
Inhale.
Exhale.
Bring your knees into your chest,
Squeeze and release.
When you feel you are ready,
open your eyes.
Slowly rise from your comfortable position,
Say the following words:
daga baki

mu duka
zo daga
zuwa baki
mun dawo
And go about your day, inspired.
My vacant flesh will disintegrate into dust.
My bones to be used as the foundation
upon which you build a home.
Should you need more like me,
we don't never die.
Barter well with the man who stole this land
and you may just get two for the price of one.

White Cube

Leila Weefur

I SEE YOU

i recognize the trauma in you that my body provokes

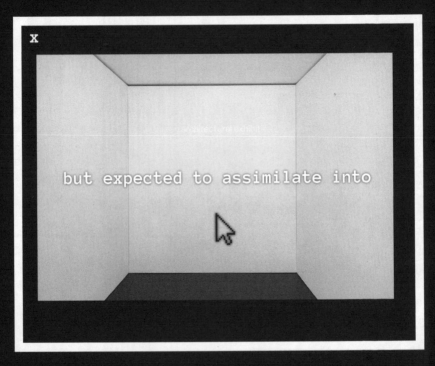

SPECT   YOUR

X

X

I AM A SPECTATOR TO YOUR FEARS
I AM A SPECTATOR TO YOUR FEARS
I AM A SPECTATOR TO YOUR FEARS
I AM A SPECTATOR TO YOUR FEARS

I AM A SPECTATOR TO YOUR FEARS
I AM A SPECTATOR TO YOUR FEARS
I AM A SPECTATOR TO YOUR FEARS
I AM A SPECTATOR TO YOUR FEARS
I AM A SPECTATOR TO YOUR FEARS

fear induced by my refusal to assimilate

I see the alliances you've formed in silence

SILENCE

silences that were crystallized in whiteness

X

WHITENESS
THAT MANIFESTED IN FORMALISM

formalism that placed your trauma in hierarc

X

x

BUT I SEE

THE FLAWS

i see the flaws the structure

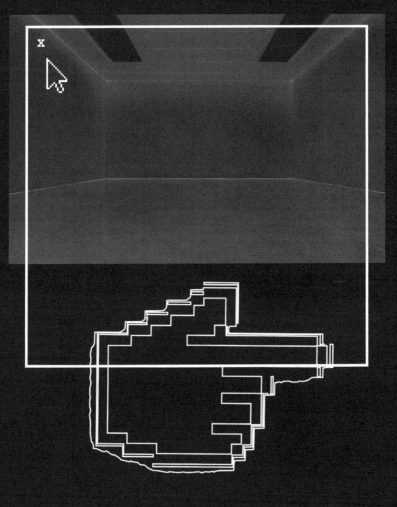

NOW, YOU SEE ME

col·lo·qui·

Vreni
Michelini
Castillo

I·isms

Please walk in a single file to your part-time job.

12 hours a week
15 hours a week
20 hours a week
35 hours a week
30 hours a week
2 hours a week
3 hours a week

–
–
–

No prep time paid
No prep time paid
No prep time paid
No prep time paid

Title: Teaching Artist
Materials: See…"the prep time is included in the hourly rate"
Dimensions: EBCPA
Year: 2015

45, 30, 35, 20, 15, 12 dollars per hour

The hourly rate does not take into consideration a living wage.
The hourly rate does not take into consideration transportation costs.
The hourly rate does not take into consideration health benefits.
The hourly rate does not take into consideration your government status.
The hourly rate does not take into consideration your
_____.
The hourly rate does not take into consideration post-traumatic colonial stress syndrome.

Title: Teaching Artist
Materials: Work for a full year with 180 children, K-6th get paid 1,600 for the entire academic year, no prep time included. We provide a free studio, rats included. You are also required to give us an additional 20 hours of volunteer time per month

including evenings and weekends.
Dimensions: Root Division
Year: 2014

Where?
The intersection[1]
between race and art
between how you're read and how you talk.

I can pass until I open my mouth

Where?
The intersection
between art and labor.

Title: Development Fellow
Materials: Can you help me fix the toilet?
Dimensions: Southern Exposure
Year: 2018

Where?
The intersection
between labor and gender.

---

1. Kimberlé Williams Crenshaw

Where?
The intersection
between art and status
between art and reparations
between art and the police state
    from Safariland to the Whitney
between art and the border
between art and the rich
    from curiosity cabinets to the Bancroft Library,
    UC Berkeley, California.

Where?
Let's just take the whole temple for our entrance
—The Met Museum, New York

P.S. Give back what you stole.

Title: Teaching Artist
Materials: Your testimony about sexual assault
cannot be considered due to the fact that you are a
contractor.
Dimensions: Youth Speaks
Year: 2016-2017

Where?
The intersection
Between art and white supremacy

Two white supremacist models

Soft
&
Hard

Title: Adjunct 1 Professor
Materials: What you earn in a semester is less than what one student pays for taking your class.
Dimensions: CCA
Year: 2017-2018

Title: Alumnx
Materials: "Thank you for all your support …the department of Painting + Printmaking works to dismantle the structural racism evidenced in our department, and create community—one that supports students of color" written by all white faculty
Dimensions: VCU
Year: 2018

Soft: A room, all white. A room, empty. They always arrive late. A poster on the door stating **Black Lives Matter.** There are no Black, full-time employees. The only Black person who worked there was an unpaid intern and X quit two months ago.

Materials: We weren't prepared to work with someone as experienced as you.
Dimensions: Southern Exposure

Soft: Five full-time employees four white.
Gallery walls white.
One full-time employee, one brown.
In a staff retreat the white Ex.Director begins to talk about equity:

What does equity mean to you?
(ASK AUDIENCE)

Ex.Director takes notes on everyone but forgets to include the only person of color in the room.

People in the room awkwardly laugh.
Hey! You forgot Y?
Y speak.
Ex. Director is not able to take notes. The discussion ends.

Next day: Y is pulled from work, thinking *wow, they might apologize for this last microaggression.* Ex.Director "you overpower group conversations." Three months ago Ex.Director screamed at Y.

Five full-time employees four white. Gallery walls white. One brown full time employee who always ends up cleaning sink. In what was once a brown neighborhood now gentrified white. Now gentrified time. Click Click.
You are welcomed here. Click Click. Facebook Link.

I come in earlier than _____.

Y leave early.
But Y you know all the right people.

Asking for a friend...
Shed impostor syndrome

Title: Teaching Artist
Materials: POC artist re-enters workspace,
curator says "What's your name again?"
We met three times already.
Dimensions: Richmond Art Center
Year: 2015-2016

Hard: POC artist hired to teach.
Interview: "You are more qualified for the lead teaching
position" Only POC in space of 16 people in total.
Curriculum turned in and accepted, two days from first class.

Title: Teaching Artist
Materials: "I know it's infused with an interesting
history and politics and whatnot, but it's a tad far
removed from these other questions/issues that you
are interested in exploring, and also, we are a visual
arts org—which sound art is a part of, but not so
much hip hop…
and also, we are visual arts org—which sound art is
apart of, but not so much hip hop…."
Dimensions: Southern Exposure
Year: 2013

Footnote: former Education Director, now works at SFMOMA.

Of course
Renée Green — *Import-Export Funk Office* (1992)

Thelma Golden — *FREESTYLE* (2001)

Thelma Golden — *FREQUENCY* (2005-6)

Thelma Golden — *FLOW* (2008)

"thinks of itself in the past, present and the future simultaneously..." — Thelma Golden

Can museums house artists and allow them...

Hard:

Hard: that percentage will always be lower for womyn of color.

Hard: Katy Perry pimping Egyptian symbols for pop song. Minute 3:00, Minute 3:18 of "Dark Horse," 2014.

Hard: Who is sitting behind the computer?

Who is standing?

There are not enough chairs.

> **Title:** Museum Preparator
> **Materials:** Preparators will have a separate party from the opening in the back of the gallery.
> **Dimensions:** YBCA
> **Year:** 2013

Asking for a friend...

Emerging
Emerging
Emerging

We are emerging. Not established.
Emerging. Emerging. Emerging.

Debt plus debt plus debt.

After how many fellowships, internships, part-time-ships do we get in?

Even then,

You are overqualified for this position.
Best wishes with your future endeavors!

A gesture that continues to infantilize.

soft _____ supremacy

I don't mean to make you uncomfortable...

Be careful of being the angry brown woman.
Be careful,
be the angry brown woman.
Appearances matter, the art world is small.
Best wishes with your future endeavors!

Raise your hand if you get paid on time.

Raise your hand if you have paid people late.

Raise your hand if you have been paid less than a minimum wage.

Raise your hand if you consistently get paid late.
(ASK AUDIENCE)

A gesture that continues to infantilize.

A gesture that continues to infantilize.

A gesture that continues to _____.
A gesture that continues to infantilize.
A gesture that continues to infantilize.

What was your name again?

Womyn of color don't have the luxury of being perceived as weak:

_____

_____

Unfortunately, the Selection Committee was not able to support your application. While I know this may come as a disappointment, I strongly encourage you to continue to look for opportunities.

Best wishes with your future endeavors!

(Cuando te falta _____
presionada por toda su cortesía).
Please don't cover your mouth
Let your racism out, at least you can recognize it.

Soul loss,
something that happens inside:
Enfrenta tus Aires del alma[2]

El Susto
El Espanto
La Tristeza
La Angustia
El Coraje
La Vergüenza
El Resentimiento
La Pena
La Envidia
Los Celos
La Culpa
El Miedo
El Egoísmo

That White Guilt

---

2. Estela Román

Rather than a specific abuse or a thread of toxic relations,
_____ is the loss,
la pérdida de algo esencial
some essential part of _____

Susto
Susto
Susto
Susto

Why are you scared of us?
Why are you scared of us?

Take some responsibility

Please don't cover your mouth.

Take
Respons

Maya
Gomez

ility

When you ask me, *Where are you from?*
and I reply, *California.*
And then you proceed to ask, *no where are you really
from?...I mean...where is your family from?*

.

In order for you to learn about my narrative, I need you to
know your own. I need you to take the time to look in the
mirror. To face our historical past, our present and our fu-
ture.

During our present day post-Obama White House era of 2018, I can't help but wonder, was it all just aesthetics? Did a Black man in the White House absolve us of our sin of omission?

For all of the times you made a decision in order to protect your position of power at the expense of someone else.
For creating and containing white institutional culture by conducting meetings where there was not one person of color in the room.
For denying our absence as a problem worthy of immediate attention.
For perpetuating the pain of any human not being seen as equal.

∎

You and your organization's executive director attend a grant information workshop that you registered for months ago. Your name is on the list, but their's is not. You ask the greeter, *is this a problem?* She responds, "probably not, but one of you will have to wait outside until all of the participants have signed in." You politely inform your boss, "you can take my spot, I'll wait outside." She says, "great, I'll save you a seat." You sit directly outside the door while she enters the room, takes a seat and begins laughing with a colleague.

You find yourself once again caught on the outside; over-looked; expendable.

Tu eres mi otro yo.
Si te hago daño a ti.
Me hago daño a mi misma.
Si te amo y respeto
*Me amo y respeto a mi.**

∎

You took a 25% pay cut from your last non-profit job, prior to taking out a $20,000 loan to pay for your master's degree. Sold into the concept of supporting an artist community in San Francisco. Your dream job. Well, at least you are getting paid and there is healthcare and vacation time. No retirement plan or designated sick leave.

But, you are doing good work and you are getting paid. Half of what the career center says your education and professional experience should be paying you. A fraction of the living wage in San Francisco, and pennies compared to all of your friends working for tech companies, but you are committed to a community and a cause.

After one year and seven months of working side by side to foster a community of artists—on your last day, you are told, *Do you mind if we cut straight to logistics?...I'll need your keys, your credit card, and your letter of resignation so that I can cut you your last check. Since it sounds like you are working today, we will pay you through the end of the day. Questions...?*

Hey, any chance there is overtime pay for the work I put into holding your hand as we navigate your borders?

.

What is your relationship to your ancestral cultural experience as an individual and as an institution?

Are you a predominantly white institution?

Why is that so difficult to say out loud?

.

For you the world is abundant, full. Your face is everywhere. She is the patron, the curator, the artist, the visitor, the director. When I look around I see, the guard, the cleaning crew, the student, the assistant, the unpaid intern. We are absent and we are abundant at the same time.

Take responsibility for our shared historical journey and the details of what happened in between 1492 and 2018 to make you walk this earth with the privileged perspective that I am the foreigner, the alien, the other.

.

Simply because your brochure uses the word equity as you print the words "claim me" on the front, does not give you permission to deny this dichotomy. The very nature of your language is inherited from the colonizer as you invite your audience to "claim you." Don't you see that you are practicing and perpetuating a paradigm of subordination, ownership and colonization regardless of what color you paint your walls?

I do not give you permission to practice on me.

*from "In Lak'ech" by Luis Valdez, 1971

Some of the worst racist tragedies in history have been perfectly legal.

–Kimberlé Williams Crenshaw

Work doesn't simply create wealth where there was only poverty before…work creates poverty, too, in direct proportion to profit.

–CrimethInc,
Ex-Workers Collective

Adding It Up

Melinda L.
de Jesús

uisa

Adding It Up: A feminist of color's herstory of working in predominantly white academic spaces[1]

Melinda L. de Jesús

1.

[1989 UCSC]   1 graduate fellowship
[1995]   1 doctorate awarded
[1995-1996 UVM] 1 disastrous diversity postdoc

[1996-1999 SFSU] First tenure track job with shitty Asian male boss and even more sexist asshole male "colleagues" who called the women of color in the college "unrelenting bitches." We promptly formed a drinking/support group called the UUB: "the Union of Unrelenting Bitches"

[1998 UGA]   1 amazing Rockefeller Summer Seminar with womanist colleagues

[1999 Stanford] 1 semester at the Center for the Study of Race and Ethnicity
                (San Francisco Supervisor Jane Kim was in my Asian American

boss but excellent colleagues

The death of my dad + divorce + Zoloft
And the best work of my life thus far, all under duress

[2000-2004]   3 Arizona-wide women of color conferences

[2003]   Getting back together with my ex

[1997-2005]   Coordinated 10 MELUS Women of Color literature caucuses

[2005-2006]   1 literature society presidency undercut by misogynist
micromanaging assholes (I sense a theme here...)

[2005]   My 40th birthday pregnancy project
My first book, *Pinay Power:Peminist Critical Theory*
Lots of conferencing and drinking
Conference travel to London and Venice

---

1   This piece was first created for the "Hot Commodities, Cheap Labor" panel at NWSA
2014, San Juan, Puerto Rico.

And a *deus ex machina* back to the Bay Area!

[2005-2006 CCA] First semester in my new job cut short by my preemie son
The surrealness of Mommylandia on full, paid leave
New classes on monsters, girl culture and boy culture

[2008-2011] My first departmental chairship

[2011-2012] Weeping as the first, then the second woman of color
boss/mentor I've ever had leave CCA after telling me,
"Get what you need, then get out!"

[2006-2009] 2 miscarriages while 10+ friends get pregnant
1 blood clotting disorder

[2009] Another truly miracle baby--a girl this time
My first stint on APT

[2010-2011] Appointed interim chair of Critical Studies while also chairing
Diversity Studies. Feeling incredibly used as the Dean (and I assume the Provost)

Organized *After Girl Power*, the first international girls studies conference, at the Centre for Women's Studies

[2009-2013] 3 controversial Diversity Studies symposiums
[2018]   1 extraordinary Diversity studies faculty exhibition entitled *Home: Making Space for Radical Love and Struggle*—but did anyone from the upper administration see it?

[2008-2011] Hired 5 faculty of color to tenure track lines
             Lost 3 of them in 7 years
             Watching the numbers of white faculty rise to almost 80% from the 69% when I was first hired in 2005.
             Is diversity really one of the college's core values?

[2014-2018] Second stint as department chair

[2014-2018] Yelled at by a red-faced, angry white woman colleague on the street right in front of the school, who sputters "You--you--faculty of color have so much power--so much!" even as we languish as chairs and middle management, never in positions of real power in faculty affairs.

Gritting my teeth as it's implied over and over that Diversity Studies should be the 6 units (my entire program!) jettisoned from the college's Gen Ed requirements

Not surprised when, speaking to the Curriculum Committee, I'm cut off when I announce that the "real problem is the school's curricular investment in white supremacy."

Trying to support three women of color faculty denied lines promised to them due to "changes in the college's vision" even as their work is lauded on the college's website as well as in print and social media around the world

[2017–2018]   6 chapbooks of political poetry
2 honorable mentions in chapbook competitions
My first full collection of poetry, *peminology*, is published
So many readings!

And yet my dean tells me he's sure my contract won't be renewed because poetry isn't "what I was hired to do;" tells my faculty I'm merely "popular"

[2018]   Finally, stepping down as chair after 7 years

bell hooks notes that "anytime we do the work of love, we do the work of ending domination"[2]

[1995-present]
For these moments of community and solidarity
sisterhood and brotherhood
To make spaces for voices unheard
For that moment of insight and clarity
That piece of advice that works
That laugh over drinks that becomes a lifeline of support
To nurture all my faculty through the eye of the needle

That's why this brown loud tenacious peminist
is still here

Dahil sa iyo[3]

---

2   bell hooks, Plenary Keynote. NWSA Annual Meeting, San Juan, Puerto Rico. November 2014.
3   Tagalog. Title of a love song, "Because of You."

for and because of all of you
    and for those yet to come

I remain.

2.

Epigraph: New Abolitionist scholar Dylan Rodriguez notes that racial apartheid and genocide are the continual condition of the academy; nevertheless he writes: radical intellectuals' inhabitation of existing institutional sites opposes structures of domination—even if, for most colonized peoples, "the academy is never home."

how do we make ourselves a/t home
in a place where
we were never wanted
a place that never imagined us inhabiting its lily white spaces
where we are meant to be the subject, never the agent
where our exclusion was/is a given
where we are merely the flavor of the month,
  the spicy sidedish
  never the main course
the guest, the ghost
  never the tenured faculty member, the department
    chair, the dean, the provost
always expected to be
  expendable
  dependable
  agreeable
and most of all
  grateful
grateful for the crumbs thrown our way
grateful to be led by white feminists (whom we can't trust)

grateful to be noticed by the white male hotshots (whom
we know to avoid)

meanwhile

we navigate this unforgiving terrain
under the white supremacist radar,
      we toil
      we conspire
      we put our "queer shoulders to the wheel"

and they
      blinded by their own masturbatory definitions of
      power
can't see that
we are planting our seeds
laying our pipeline
making family
creating community
nurturing alliances
learning from one another
casting our net wide
our righteousness
our love and struggle
change this game
change it
      into something bigger
far beyond the game itself
      (not mere art for art's sake)

our histories ground us
our ancestors guide us
to this higher plane
transformed
we will become
       we have become
the future
we've been longing for

August 7, 2018
Dedicated in love and struggle to all of my allies in my 23
years in academia.
MAKIBAKA!

Ruminati on Labor

Jen Everett

ns

WE ARE
NEVER NOT WORKING
EVERYTHING IS ~~####~~ TRANSACTIONAL
AM I SHAKING THE RIGHT HANDS
~~####~~ WORKING THE RIGHT ROOMS?
DON'T LIVE ON EITHER COAST
WILL THE WORK BE SEEN?

I'M NOT YOUNG ENOUGH TO BE AN
IT GIRL LAUGH
I DON'T ~~####~~ AFTER EVERY SENTENCE
I ONLY SMILE WHEN I MEAN IT
I STOPPED LISTENING AFTER THAT
WEAK HANDSHAKE
I (WON'T) LABOR ~~########~~ ON YOUR
BEHALF ——————→ NOT EMOTIONALLY,
                 NOT PHYSICALLY
                 NOT INTELLECTUALLY
UR LACK OF RIGOR IS DISAPPOINTING
EXPECTED MORE

SEE
SUPPORT
CURATE
COLLECT MY WORK WHEN BLACKNESS
AND QUEERNESS AREN'T ON TREND

A BLACK WOMAN VISIT MY STUDIO?
E GATHER WITHOUT THREATENING

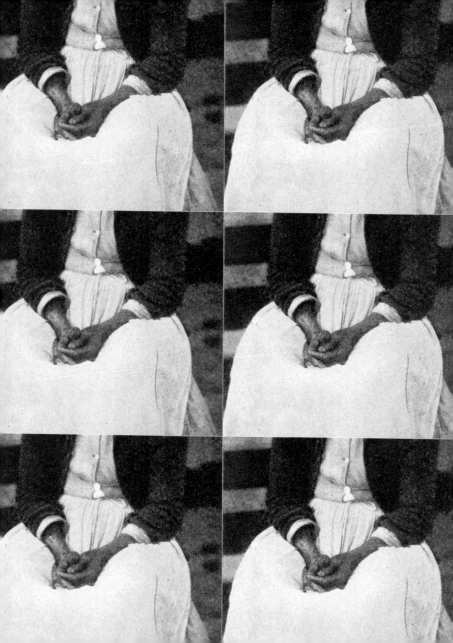

We are never not workin

But we will not labor o

Labor is physical, inte
me for any and all of i

See, support, collect &
blackness and queerness

our behalf.

ctual, emotional. Pay

rate my work when
en't on trend.

White Boards

Keara Gray

These blank white boards .
Waiting for me to put the color on
them . I am the one who makes
the art .
I take the plain and add the flavor .
Me . This women of color .
Where is my white board ?
May I trade it in for a black one ?
Only these white boards getting
turned into art . Waiting for me to
put the color on them .
These white boards need me !
They need my color !
Because I am the one who adds
the flavor .

I am the one who makes the art .

These white boards without color .

They ain't nothing .

THEY NEED ME .

They need my flavor . The curves I
put on them . The zigzags I add to
my lines .

They think they can go without my
color . They ain't nothing without it .

THEY NEED ME . My flavor .

My art .

I wonder to myself . When will
my color by appreciated on these
white boards .

Because they NEED me. I am the
one who ADDS the FLAVOR .
I am the one who MAKES the ART

.

Welcome

Nasim Aghili

Note to self:
Stay with your body! Remember all the things they've told
you before so you can avoid being left alone with experi-
ence of shame, abandonment, distress, failure, grief and
disorientation.

"Välkommen!"
"Välkommen det här är vår teater. Letar du efter nåt?"
"Välkommen. Vi är så stolta över att du är här. Vi inser att vi
behöver lite färg."
"Välkommen till vår arbetsplats. Vi är så glada att du är här.
Förra veckan hade vi en föreläsning om mångfald."
"Välkommen det här är vår arbetsplats. Ja vi är alla vita. Men
du är ju här nu. Kan vi ta ett kort på dig när du ler?"

"Welcome!"
"Welcome this is our theatre. Can I help you?"
"Welcome. We are so proud having you here. We realize
we need colour."

"Welcome to our work space. We are so happy you are here. Last week we had a lecture about diversity."
"Welcome this is our work space. Yes we are all white. But you are here now. Can we take a picture of you smiling?"

"Ja vi är alla vita."
"Ja vi är alla vita. Är du säker på att du inte frågade mig nåt om vithet?"
"Ja vi är alla vita. Men vi jobbar på det."
"Ja vi är alla vita. Vi har jobbat jättemycket med vår vithet och det faktum att alla är vita."
"Ja vi är alla vita. På såna här institutioner är alla anställda vita. Vi jobbar jättehårt med att reflektera kring vår vithet och våra privilegier."

"Yes we are all white"
"Yes we are all white. You're sure you didn't ask me something about whiteness?"
"Yes we are all white. But we are working on it."
"Yes we are all white. We have been working a lot with our whiteness and the fact that everyone is white."
"Yes we are all white. In institutions like this all employees are white. We are working really hard reflecting about our whiteness and our privileges."

"Hej jag ringer dig för vi letar efter en konstnär som har andra historier att berätta."
"Hej jag ringder dig för att vi behöver konstnärer med unika,

intressanta erfarenheter som kan hjälpa våra anställda konstnärer att bli mer villiga att berätta andra historier."

"Hej jag ringer dig men jag vet inte mycket om ditt arbete eller din kompetens eller din konstnärliga praktik men jag har hört att du inte är en sån där aggressiv en.

"Hej jag ringer dig för att fråga om du vill göra en oavlönad föreläsning om vithet."

"Hej jag ringer dig för att jag har en kompis som såg dig göra en föreläsning om vithet eller mångfald eller nåt sånt där."

"Hi I'm calling you since we are looking for artists with other stories to tell."

"Hi I'm calling you since we need help from artists with unique, interesting experiences to help our paid artists to be more open to tell other stories."

"Hi I'm calling you but I don't know much about your work or your competence or your artistic practice but I've heard you are not one of the aggressive ones."

"Hi I'm calling you to ask if you would like to do a free lecture about whiteness."

"Hi I'm calling you cause I have a friend that saw your lecture about whiteness or diversity or something like that."

Note to self:
Read Sara Ahmed over and over again.

Note to sister:
Let's sit in a circle and read Sara Ahmed out loud. She

defines our pain through the term <u>arriving</u>. She encourages us to be independent by not participating in their <u>happy diversity</u>. She defines the dehumanization of us through descriptions of <u>white institutions with feelings</u>.

"Jag känner ett jättestort obehag när du pratar så där."
"Jag känner nästan ångest när du säger såna där saker."
"Jag känner mig väldigt ledsen när du pratar om rasism."
"Jag känner mig ouppskattad när du inte ser och bekräftar allt arbete jag gör kring min vithet."
"Jag känner mig väldigt attackerad när du pratar både om rasism och om mig i samma mening."

"I feel very uncomfortable when you talk like that."
"I feel very anxious when you say things like that."
"I feel very sad when you talk about racism."
"I feel very unappreciated when you don't acknowledge the work I'm doing around my whiteness."
"I feel very attacked when you talk about racism and about me in the same sentence."

"Alla som jobbar här är så privilegierade."
"Alla som jobbar här är så vita."
"Alla som jobbar här är så medel (över) klass."
"Alla som jobbar här saknar erfarenhet av rasism."
"Alla som jobbar här har en fast inkomst."

"Everyone working here is so privileged."
"Everyone working here is so white."
"Everyone working here is so middle (upper) class."

"Everyone working here lacks experiences of racism."
"Everyone working here has a regular income."

"Välkomna!"
"Välkomna det här är vår teater."
"Välkomna kan jag ta ett kort på er när ni ler?"
"Välkomna kan ni snälla bara stiga åt sidan lite för vi väntar på några konstnärer."
"Välkomna och snälla var inte så arga och upprörda bara för att jag inte insåg att just ni är konstnärerna."

"Welcome!"
"Welcome this is our theatre."
"Welcome can I take a picture of you smiling?"
"Welcome can you please step aside cause we are waiting for artists."
"Welcome and please don't be so angry and aggressive just because I didn't realize that a group of you people actually were the artists."

Note to self:
Don't tell them it's not for them.
Don't tell them your purpose is not encouraging their empathy for poor people of colour.
Don't ask for more money than they offer cause they will tell you all the reasons why you are not worth it.
Don't tell them you got another threat from white supremacists cause they will cry and tell you that they feel uncomfortable not being able to do something about it.
Don't offend the journalist who's crying and tells you that

they "can't even imagine living like that" when you are talking about your everyday life.

Don't make the manager understand you have experienced racism in their institution cause they will first look indignant and then punish you in every way possible.

Don't ask about the same healthcare benefits as the others cause then you will find out that the institution sees you as someone without needs.

Don't talk about the institution's methods for making you work as though you are a super human cause then you will realize they don't think you are human.

Note to sister:
Let's hold hands when we enter the building.
Let me hold your hand when my body is looking for orientation in a room that embodies whiteness as the point for orientation.

Note to self:
Don't wipe their tears.

Note to sister:
Please bring the sage.

Note to self:
Don't abandon your body when it evokes a lot of white feelings and rage.

"Ja jag tjänar mer pengar än du men jag måste faktiskt betala min hyra."

"Ja jag behöver krismöte när jag är ledsen men har rätt att vägra dig hjälp när du får dödshot."

"Ja jag är den riktiga konstnären och du bara en del av vår mångfaldsplan."

"Ja jag tycker att jag är färgblind men att du inte är det."

"Ja jag är faktiskt trött på att du klagar hela tiden när jag har öppnat dörrarna till den här viktiga institutionen."

"Yes I earn much more than you but I actually have to pay my rent."

"Yes I need an emergency meeting when I feel sad but have the right to deny you help when you get life threats."

"Yes I am the real artist and you are just a part of our diversity quota."

"Yes I think I'm colour blind and that you are not."

"Yes I'm sick of you complaining all the time when I actually have opened the door to this great institution."

"Fast du är här nu."

"Fast nu när du är här kan du inte gärna kalla oss rasister."

"Fast alla tjänar ju på att du arbetar gratis med att utbilda oss om våra privilegier."

"Fast jag antar att det inte bara är jag utan också du som är intresserad av en mer rättvis konstproduktion och representation."

"Fast jag fick för mig att vi alla hade samma mål att skapa en bättre värld där jag kan behålla mina privilegier och betrakta ditt leende foto på min vägg och känna mig god, unik, förstående och i samklang med den samtid och värld jag kontrollerar."

"Well you are here now."
"Well now that you are here you can't call us racists."
"Well it's best for everyone if you work for free educating us about our privileges."
"Well I guess not only me but also you are interested in a more equal art production and representation."
"Well I thought we all had the same goal of creating a better world, where I can keep my privileges and look at your smiling picture on my wall, and feel so good, so unique, so understanding, so in tune with the time and the world that I control."

Note to self:
Never let our struggle be defined by the ones who sleep on soft, dry pillows every night. Never let our desires be named by the full bellies that never had to choose between children to feed. Never let our dreams be talked about by the bodies that never had the need to fake identities, shred passports, hide documents or look for new names.

Note to sister:
But please let us braid each other's hair. Cause it's possible for us to only want each other's approval. Cause we are the ones that allow each other to tell stories we recognize.

We are the ones that share the recourse and reject power. We are the ones able to live a sisterhood that includes every sister agreeing to share the burden of that struggle and having the courage to enjoy the fruits of that labour.

In the Quiet Dignity:

Black Womxn, Art and Knowledge Production

shah noor hussein

"Only the black woman can say 'when and where I enter, in the quiet, undisputed dignity of my womanhood, without violence and without suing or special patronage, then and there the whole…race enters with me.'"
—Anna Julia Cooper (1892)

BURSTING FROM THE MARGINS:
LANGUAGE AND MUSIC

foundations: one

> I don't remember
> When I learned to write but
> Somewhere between five and seven years old
> I was given a journal
> For my so many buzzing thoughts
> And baba said I 'should have somewhere to put them'
>
> *"but what should i write about, baba?"*
> 'Everything'

For me, speaking and writing came nearly simultaneously; I don't remember constructing words without a visual script for accompaniment. As a child my father encouraged my vocal tendencies by insisting that I document more of what I had to say through the language of writing. Growing older, I learned to experiment with written language, varying my composition between prose and poetry, introducing multisyllabic words at every opportunity and playfully varying my syntax. To a certain extent, I "mastered" the language of writing; in particular, I had mastered the *master's* written language, English. It was not until my young adulthood, as I forged my identity through the trials of my undergraduate program, I began to have a dialogue with the English language that didn't assume it's absolute power and unscrutinized rightness. During this period of transition, I turned to the works of feminist and womanist scholars for guidance, and during my masters program discovered *Teaching to Transgress*, a book of essays by bell hooks, and read chapter eleven, entitled "Language." Here, hooks writes on the power English held over "enslaved Africans" and admits that "only as a woman did I begin to think about these black people in relation to language, to think about their trauma as they were compelled to witness their language rendered meaningless with a colonizing European culture, where their voices where deemed foreign, renegade speech."[1]

foundations: two

My first in class poetry assignment
Must have been second or third grade

We make little books of poems
And I write one about mama

Mama and i
Our love in this book

Reading it out loud to her
In our living room after receiving an A plus

And so nervous
That I didn't look up

So scared she wouldn't understand my poetic
    language
That was not in her native tongue

And maybe slightly ashamed
Of this truth

And so nervous
That I didn't look up

Until the end

To see her crying
And smiling

To meet her eyes
And discover them wet

And alive

Despite their suffering, hooks describes the efforts taken by
African Americans to reclaim their use of English. She notes
that through our restructuring of the grammar and syntax of
English, black folks took control of the language that had
taken them so far away from home.

*Learning English, learning to speak the alien tongue,
was one way enslaved Africans began to reclaim
their personal power within a context of domination.*

*Possessing a shared language, black folks could
find again a way to make community, and a means
to create the political solidarity necessary to resist. In
the mouths of Black Africans in the so-called 'New
World,' enslaved black people took broken bits of
English and made them a counter-language. Often,
the English used in the song reflected the broken,
ruptured world of the slaves…And even as eman-
cipated black people sang spirituals, they did not
change the language, the sentence structure, of our
ancestors. For in the incorrect usage of words, in the
incorrect placement of words, was a spirit of rebellion
that claimed language as a site of resistance."* [2]

In my creative writing, personal dialogues, and academic
research, I pursue an investigation of language reclama-
tion—specifically those efforts taken on by black women
and which remain resonant in the lives of black folks today.
When bell hooks discusses the "spirit of rebellion" pres-
ent within African American holy music, I am immediately
reminded of the R&B and rap music of today and how it
serves as the gospel. This seems fitting, since it was hooks
who states that "in contemporary black popular culture, rap
music has become one of the spaces where black vernac-
ular speech is used in a manner that invites mainstream
culture to listen —to hear—and, to some extent, be trans-
formed."
Dr. Andreana Clay, a sociologist and researcher on hip-hop
feminism, has written papers that link queer black culture,

music and social justice, including writings on Meshell Ndegeocello. Ndegeocello is an R&B and hip hop artist who is openly bisexual and presents with a gender fluid style, whose music and lyrics speak to the themes of "social protest and sexuality."[4]. Narratives of poverty, homelessness, unemployment, racial identity, white hegemonic beauty standards and self-sustainability in social justice work appear in the rapper's work, filtered through the lens of her queer identity.[5] The articulation of these complex topics and social issues within the language of popular culture is akin to the packaging of wisdom in the form of poetic language, such as proverbs to folk culture to slave shanties, which (re) appear in the rhythmic flows of black music and rap songs.

PERFORMING THEORY:
BLACK, QUEER, RESILIENT

We write from every different place,
To reclaim our names, and inherited legacies we want to
*   pass along.*
We write to stay in places as we choose –
We who crossed the Atlantic all those yesterdays ago,
We who have come again today –
We who have stayed in place through generations,
We who will stay in place tomorrow –
We are the tomorrow our grandmothers dreamed
We are grandmothers dreaming other tomorrows.
—Abena P.A. Busia, 2010

Dr. Clay also focuses her discussion on the glaring lack of publicity Ndegeocello and other queer and lesbian women in hip-hop received, including the limited airplay Ndegeocello was given on mainstream hip-hop stations even while she gained commercial success and acceptance. She states that "Ndegeocello's marginal status in the Black community is similar to the historical and collective experience of Black queer and lesbian women."[6] Patrick Johnson, a scholar of African American and performance studies, makes a similar argument grounded in both theoretical concepts and anecdotal evidence. He offers a theory of Black Queer Performance as a tool for reading these phenomena by claiming that Queer Theory does not adequately interpret "black cultural aesthetics."[7] Johnson's "theory of performance" is deployed as Quare Studies, which "points to how acts [or performances] are historically situated" and related to social and cultural experiences.[8] He uses Quare Studies to dismantle the notions of "black authenticity" that limit "blackness" to working class communities, darker hues, southern accents, heterosexuality, and hegemonic masculinity by asserting that these are "no more signifiers of blackness" than their counter-traits.[9]

Linking these concepts, we can see that Clay, Ndegeocello and Johnson would agree that white institutions cannot hold the full complexity of black identity, therefore leaving the complex and queer further displaced to the margins. This is why Johnson's theory of performance does what these spaces cannot, by "neither dissolving identity into a fixed 'I' nor presuming a monolithic, 'we'" but rather attempts to find a balance.[10] Quare Studies calls on a performed knowledge that is both collective and communal, coming from shared culture and ancestry, while simultaneously acknowledging the diversity of individual experiences. This diversity of experience is expressed in Clay's work, Ndegeocello's art and queer black women's lives as we tackle many intersecting issues through our layered identities. This centers queer black life as the "symbolic [space] of an emerging critical discourse on Black women, queer identity, and sexual politics" which aims to "challenge popular representations of women of color" and "articulate the persistence of racism and sexism" in both art and academic institutions.[11]

Johnson lists some methods for challenging the whiteness of art and institutions, calling on them the "performance strategies of African Americans" that comprise his theory of performed knowledge.[12] Stemming from the "vernacular traditions that emerged among enslaved Africans," they include "folktales, spirituals, and the blues," as well as representations of Black Queer resiliency modeled in "discursively mediated forms" such as "vogueing, snapping, 'throwing shade,' and 'reading.'"[13] These modern (re)enactments and (re)embodiments of ancestral performance "attest to the ways in which gays, lesbians, bisexuals, and transgender people of color devise technologies of self-assertion and summon the agency to resist."[14] Have you ever thrown subtle shade at white co-workers, perhaps couched in a timely gaze towards the only other person of color or black person in the room? Have you ever vogued in a predominantly white club in an effort to take space and assert your presence? Ever loudly snapped at a poetry reading or hooted at a karaoke night? Have you ever read a room, person or space for your safety or radical pleasure? This is discursive black queer performance as resilience.

In his closing, Johnson calls Quare Studies "'bi'-directional" claiming that "it theorizes from bottom to top and top to bottom" while "keeping in mind that political theory and political action are not necessarily mutually exclusive."[15] This critical discourse points toward an aspect of embodied knowing that emerges out of queer black womens' experiences living on the margins. Stephanie Y. Mitchem, professor of theology and women's studies, calls these lived experiences "culturally accumulated" knowledges that Black people have collected throughout the diaspora and have, therefore, become a "part of the knowledge base on [and from] which black women and men—consciously or not—draw in daily living."[16] Mitchem believes that Black women's positionality and historical exclusion from professional careers and fields, including universities and elite art spaces such as museums and galleries, has placed them in a position from which they can access and produce subversive forms of knowledge.[17] Therefore, Johnson's "summoning" of this "interventionist disciplinary project" appropriately recognizes alternative ways of knowledge production and reproduction, particularly those embodied in the performed knowledges of African American queers and women.[18]

foundations: three

A dream
                    About warrior me
                                    Caring for mama
                        missing baba
writing a book
                    kissing my ancestors
                                    living in their home
                    living in their names
and approval.

NUE AMERICA:
CAPITAL AND PRECARITY

I.
White man say
That there is no more daily wage
That now we have monthly salaries
That workers are stable
And maybe happy

Feburary 15, 2018

Dear ████▌

A decision has been made regarding your admission to the
University of ████████ ███████ ███████████████▌
████▌ you will need need to log back into your application
to view this decision. You may access your status page
here.

Best,
Graduate Admissions
██████████▌
Vice Provost for Graduate Studies and
Dean of the Graduate Division
University of ████████████████▌

5.4/5.0 This incoming message has been identified by the
████ central filters as spam. This attachment is provid-

ed so that you can review the reasons the message was tagged. If you have further questions please email ithelp@ ███████edu for assistance. Content analysis details: (5.4 points, 5.0 required)

pts	rule name	description
2.5	FSL_HELO_NON_FQDN_1	FSL_HELO_NON_FQDN_1
0.5	DCC_CHECK	Detected as bulk mail by DCC (dcc-servers.net)
1.3	RDNS_NONE	Delivered to internal network by a host with no rDNS
0.0	FSL_BULK_SIG	Bulk signature with no Unsubscribe

II.
White man say
That there is no more daily wage
That now we have monthly salaries
That workers are stable
And maybe happy

March 5, 2018

Dear ███████████████

It is with regret that we write to inform you that you have not been accepted for graduate study at the University of

The materials you submitted with your application have been carefully reviewed by the admissions committee, but we are unable to offer you admission.

The ███████████ campus has a strict enrollment ceiling, and we are thus very limited in the number of new students we may admit each year. The admissions committee has the difficult task of selecting students with the strongest overall records from a large pool of well-qualified applicants. Unfortunately, this may result in not being able to accept many applicants who are capable of excellent academic work.

We appreciate the interest you have shown in ███████████ and wish you success in achieving your academic goals.

Sincerely,

███████████

III.
Does white man see
Does white man see
Does white man see
Does white man see
Does white man see
Does white man see
Does white man see?

February 4, 2018

Dear █████

Thank you for applying to the University of ████████ for graduate study. Your application has been carefully reviewed by the Graduate Admissions Committee of the Cultural Studies graduate program and by the Office of Graduate Studies. I regret to inform you that your application for graduate study at ████████ was not approved. The program to which you applied indicated the following as the reason(s) that you were not selected for admission:

No additional space available in the graduate program for this admissions cycle.

If you have any questions regarding the reasons for your denial, you may contact the admissions advisor of the Cultural Studies graduate program. If in the future you believe that your accomplishments may be competitive, please do not hesitate to reapply. I wish you every success in achieving your educational objectives.

Sincerely,

████████████

Dean -- Graduate Studies
Vice Provost -- Graduate Education

IV.
Does white man see the recent college grads
Overschooled and underemployed

Teaching and artist and freelance and contract
And every day
Hoping to please some white man
In order to be given workplace assignments
Today or tomorrow
For a week
Or two

March 15th, 2018

Dear █████████████

I regret to inform you that your application for admission
to graduate standing at the University of ████████████
████ has not been approved.

The number of well-qualified applicants for admission to
graduate study at ████████ far exceeds the number of
places available. Although a substantial majority of these
applicants will meet every minimal standard an admissions
committee might establish, not all will actually be admitted.
Admission nearly always depends on, for example, compat-
ibility of the applicant's expressed interests with those of
faculty in the program, and balance of disciplinary subfields
within the program, as well as other factors. Please direct
any further inquiry you might have to the Department to
which you applied.

Although it has not proved possible for us to offer you a

place, we sincerely appreciate your interest in the ███████ ███████ campus of the ████████████████. I wish you well in your current and future pursuit of advanced studies.

Sincerely,

████████████
Vice Provost and Dean of Graduate Studies

V.
Are these workers stable?
Does their money come as a monthly salary
Deposited neatly into their checking account?
Have these workers seen the so-called benefits
Of the transformation of wage work?
Have they been permitted to move up
In the system they will say is evolving?

March 20th, 2018

Dear ████████████████

Your application for graduate study in Ethnic Studies at the University of ████████████████ has been carefully reviewed. We regret to inform you that you have not been selected for admission.

A number of factors are considered in evaluating each application. Please be aware that ████████████ receives a large number of applications and many excellent candidates could not be offered admission. Unfortunately, we are only able to extend offers to a limited number of qualified applicants.

If you have questions about the decision you may contact the program to which you applied directly. Program contact information can be found at ████████████████████ ████████. Please note that some departments are unable to respond to such requests due to the large volume of applications received.

Thank you for your interest in the University of ████████ ████████. An official letter has been posted on the Application Status page of your ████████ application at ████████████████████. I wish you the best in all your endeavors.

Sincerely,

████████████

Dean of the Graduate Division
University of ████████████████
"Graduate education that transforms, enriches, and inspires"

VI.
White man say
That there is no more daily wage
That now we have monthly salaries
That workers are stable

And maybe happy

Does white man see
Does white man see?

White man chooses not to see.

GLOSSARY OF TERMS: A QUEER BLACK FEMINIST PERSPECTIVE

nonprofit: non · prof · it
/nän'präfit/
> *Adjective*
> not for profit; not oriented to or driven towards bearing profit
> *Noun*
> an entity, institution or collective that operates for social good (not profit); mission based
> related: charity, foundation

art:
/ärt/
> *Noun*
> creative projects, productions or works typically in visual or written forms
> the expression of creativity and imagination channeled through practiced or learned skill
> relating to or critical of aesthetics, beauty, social life, culture and history

academic: ac · a · dem · ic
/akə'demik/
> *Adjective*
> (a person) within an institution of higher education and learning
> (a course or study) conducted and supported through frameworks and theories; peer-reviewed

(an art) practiced under a tradition or within a lineage; formalized - see: ritual

industrial: in · dus · tri · al
/inˈdəstrēəl/
>*Adjective*
>related to or characterized by industries, systems and processes
>large in scale, extent and operations; overdeveloped
>noisy, harsh, uncompromising; see - oppressive

complex: com · plex
/kämˈpleks,kəmˈpleks,ˈkäm‚pleks/
>*Adjective*
>consisting of many interlocking or moving parts; difficult to understand
>buildings or structures serving a similar purpose or sharing a similar location; a network
>involving both real and imaginary parts; intricate

FOOTNOTES

1. hooks, 168; 2. hooks, 170; 3. hooks, 171; 4. Clay, 59; 5. Clay, 61-68;
6. Clay, 59; 7. Johnson, 5; 8. Johnson, 10; 9. Johnson, 14 - 16;
10. Johnson, 15; 11. Clay, 69; 12. Clay, 12; 13. Johnson, 13;
14. Johnson, 13; 15. Johnson, 18-19; 16. Johnson, 33; 17. Johnson, 34;
18. Johnson, 20

WORKS CITED

Busia, Abena P.A. "A Song in Seven Stanzas for Our Granddaughters," in *African Women Writing Resistance: An Anthology of Contemporary Voices*, edited by Jennifer Browdy de Hernandez, Pauline Dongala, Omotayo Jolaosho, and Anne Serafin, xix – xxi. University of Wisconsin Press, 2010.

hooks, bell. "Language: Teaching New Worlds / New Words," in *Teaching to Transgress: Education as the Practice of Freedom*, 167 – 177. New York: Routledge, 2014.

Clay, Andreana. *Like an Old Soul Record: Black Feminism, Queer Sexuality, and the Hip-Hop Generation* in Meridians: feminism, race, transnationalism 8 (1): 53-73. http://muse.jhu.edu/journals/mer/summary/v008/8.1clay.html, 2007

Johnson, E. Patrick. "Quare Studies, or (Almost) Everything I Know About Queer Studies I Learned from My Grandmother," in *Black Queer Studies: A Critical Anthology,* 124 –153. Durham, NC: Duke University Press, 2005.

Mitchem, Stephanie Y. "'There is a Balm...' Spirituality & Healing among African American Women." *Michigan Family Review* 7.1, 2002.

We all owe to the cosmic order, and it is impossible, at this level, to do for others what others are expected to do for themselves.

–Malidoma Patrice Somé

Que aire te pico?…Hay que,
hacer pues, los trabajos
necesarios para que el aire,
nos permita seguir nuestro
camino.

–Estela Román

LANDSCAPE

Speaking Myself

Shylah Pacheco Hamilton

For

Speaking for myself, most of the time, people look right through me.
They think I am the student, not a professor.

I entered the faculty lounge, using my faculty identification to unlock the door, and found it nearly empty.
There was one lone woman, who looked me up and down and smiled curiously.
I returned the smile as I settled at a table, preparing for my upcoming class.

"Hi," the woman said.
"Hello," I replied.
"This is the faculty space, is there something I can help you with?"

"Yes, I am aware this is the faculty space and no, I am fine, but thank you."
I then had to introduce myself, as faculty, to this woman who thought I was lost and taking up space in the faculty lounge. I could only enter the room, if I had a faculty ID. This fact, for some reason, escaped her.

Women that look like me are few and far between in academia.
Blame historical and racial disparities, there are usually only a few of us on the tenure-track.
I have experienced these episodes more times than I can count. I am often mistaken for other African-descended women on campus, most of whom work as non-managerial staff members.
Hardwired to protect white spaces, these folks are ignorant, but that is no excuse.

I hope these folks know I do not represent every woman of color.
I hope these folks know I do not have all the answers.
I hope these folks know I am not the expert on "race."
I hope these folks know I am not to be exoticized.
I hope these folks know I will reclaim my time.
I hope these folks know I am not the one.
I hope these folks know not to act a fool on a day when I have time.
I hope these folks know I will call them out.
They don't know I have armies of Egun on all sides.

I can only speak for myself, but Sandy continues to speak for all of us.

I never met Sandy Bland. But I miss her.

Sandra Annette Bland was born on February 7, 1987 in Naperville, Illinois.

Sister Sandy was leaving Prairie View A&M University after accepting a job when she was assaulted by a police officer, arrested, jailed and assassinated while in police custody. But you know that already.

> I recall one of her early videos, where she survived a car crash. A motorcycle crashed into her car, embedded itself in her back window. The motorcyclist survived. Sandy cried and praised God that they both lived. For her, it was evidence of God's grace. Less than four months later, she would be dead. Eclipsed right out of our lives.

I can only speak for myself but I was not born into a fair system.

I was born into a system where my opportunities were solely determined by my native language, race, religion, gender and zip code.

I was raised by my grandmother, who spoke Spanish, did not graduate from high school, cursed the texture of my hair and taught me how to make tortillas.

I loved books.

I loved art.

I loved nature.

My little brother is more comfortable in prison and on drugs than lucid and on the outside.
My older brother moved away and passes for "Hispanic."
My oldest sister did not live to see 21.
But here I am, fighting for legitimacy, in protected white spaces.
Telling my daughters, "YOU TOO CAN INFILTRATE."
Here I am, making my family proud, not knowing what I don't know.
Recognizing that I don't know what I don't know.
Wishing I had someone in my family to call to find out what I don't know.
Hoping it won't be too detrimental to me as I find my way to the answers.
I deserve to have a creative life of the mind, just as much as anyone.
I made this an option when it wasn't presented as an option to me.
I'm grateful.

I can only speak for myself but June continues to speak for all of us.
June Millicent Jordan was born on July 9th, 1936 in Harlem, NY.
Mama June died from breast cancer, after fighting the University of California at Berkeley for her rightful health insurance benefits.

> Before she died, she read from a poem in which
> she imagined her dying body and a predatory hawk

gliding overhead: "He makes that dive / to savage / me / and inches / from the blood flood lusty / beak / I roll away / I speak / I laugh out loud / Not yet / big bird of prey / not yet."

Indeed. Not yet, big bird of prey. Not yet.

Making Memory Visible:

A conversation with Celia Herrera Rodríguez

Visual artist Celia Herrera Rodríguez (Xicana/O'dami) is a painter, performance and installation artist whose work reflects a full generation of dialogue with Xicana, Native American, Pre-Columbian, and Mexican thought. She considers herself a working artist, embracing her role in community as an organizer and a teacher, actively exhibiting her work, and continuing to create new work in her studio.

The conversation that follows took place along the 5 FWY while Cherríe Moraga drove us back to Santa Barbara after spending five days with one another in San Diego for Un Llanto Colectivo—a two-day ceremonial performance protest along the U.S. Mexico border, against the separation of families and in support of the Caravanas.

We reflected on the performance and then listened to Vreni's piece "colloquialisms" the seed we sent out as a call to all contributors.

Maya: When did you begin to call yourself an artist, in public, to friends, family, and what were their reactions?

Celia: I first began to call myself an artist when I was nine. I did it in school, amongst my classmates and teachers. My friends all accepted this declaration, because we were all kids and everything no matter how strange might be possible. I remember in my eighth grade yearbook one of my friends (Charlie) wrote, and I remember it because it made me laugh, "that I would probably be one of the artists drawing *Archie* Comic Books," which is not far from what I do.

When, I told my grandmother, she thought it was out of the blue, as if it were something bizarre, something way beyond my means. I think she understood it as something only rich people could do. My grandmother spent her time working hard to support us. She worked in restaurants - cooking, washing dishes; at the canneries; and washing clothes. Into her seventies, she worked as a domestic worker for middle class white folks and a caretaker for the elderly in our community. While she was working, I filled my time alone, reading, drawing and spending time in my imagination. My drawing at that time was what my mom called monigotes and garabatos.

Maya: So, you declared yourself an artist at nine and you continued...

Celia: I'm blessed that way. I get to do what I imagined I would do - make art and teach. I found teaching, because as a child, I had this idea that art was very personal, and it could bring me a lot of joy, but for me, it was very private, and I needed to do something that would be of service to society.

Maya: What are some of the contradictions that you grapple with in your own practice as an artist and in life?

Celia: One, is that I don't teach painting, but I do teach within Chicano Studies, the concepts and the history behind art - even though I have an MFA in painting.

Since I was young, I had a certain life in school and a certain life at home with very little adult supervision. I was raised by my grandmother, because my mother died when I was very young. I thought of myself as independent and spent a lot of time alone. I became very rebellious and autonomous like my grandmother. I knew I had to have *freedom*, because that is how I grew up—my grandmother provided that for me in many ways. She made it possible for me to have this interior space which I wanted to pursue; and after high school I decided that I would go to college and study art.

In elementary school, the nuns taught us that a person had to have a purpose that was bigger

Photographs of Un Llanto Colectivo Jeff Valenzuela, 2018

than oneself. So when I became aware of the Chicana/o Movement as I entered college at CSU Sacramento, I was primed for it. I knew I needed to work in community and as an artist, I just didn't yet know what that would look like. I encountered my first Chicana/o art teachers, Jose Montoya and Esteban Villa, they took us (me and fellow students) back into *my* community where I grew up. This intervention allowed me to see my experience through their eyes. They taught me to understand my history as part of a larger history.

So, for me, the contradiction always was, how do

you serve in community? and how do you have this private life of the mind? and this space that allows you to imagine?

Maya: What experiences helped you develop as an artist?

Celia: I left home at seventeen to go to college, after I had my daughter, but I left after two semesters, once I realized that I was too young. I also became very interested in the Chicana/o Movement, the rise of the movements shaped my ideas and views of the world I was living in at the time.

I was recruited to go to Cuba on the Venceremos Brigade in 1971. The 'cadre training' (preparations to spend two months working in Cuba) included readings and discussions on the relevant topics of the day: colonialism, imperialism, labor history, women's rights, history of the Americas… this provided a context for me to understand my own Mexican family's experience.

I spent time in meetings with organizations fighting for social justice like the Farmworkers, the struggle to save the International Hotel in San Francisco, the fight to retain Grove Street College in Oakland. These meetings were coupled with collective work projects in Oakland, San Francisco, Berkeley and Delano. When I left college, I put artmaking on hold and worked in the Movement.

After returning from Cuba, I went to live in New York. I spent time in Puerto Rico and worked in

Los Angeles for a social justice organization as an organizer and an advocate defending the rights of undocumented workers and families in the United States.

It was not until I was pregnant with my second child that I returned home to Sacramento and decided it was time to go back to school and study art. It was the time spent in the Chicana/o movement that introduced me to the major artist and art organizations of the time.

I also spent time with friends who were working with Teatro Campesino and attended their women's group. I went to Mexico and spent time with The Mascarones and then Teatro Zerol. Through watching theatre artists, I learned how to work and live as an artist and how to think about myself working in the arts as an intellectual. I was interested in the collective work of making art, but I could not find my place in it as most spaces were male dominated. At the time the focus was painting murals, silkscreening public and political statements—I did not feel very skillful in these areas, so I just kept studying, raising my kids, and engaging in the cultural, spiritual and political life of my community.

I also began teaching, doing the work that Vreni is talking about in "colloquialisms." Doing work in different capacities with youth and with elders - It really had nothing to do with getting paid for

it—those years that I was in school and learning to live and work as an artist, I was supported in part by the state welfare system. That was the primary financial support during that time. I could not have gone to school, nor developed a practice as a thinker and an artist without that support. The majority of my young friends with children lived as I did. So I say to those that malign folks in the welfare system, that system produced many fine thinkers and activists that spent their youth working to make positive changes in all aspects of society.

Maya: How did your role as a mother impact your work as an artist?

I had my third child by the time I was 24 years old. The kids were my entire family! They were and continue to be the motivating factor of my life experience as much so as my education and my desire to make art. They were in the Movement with me, they were the reason I sought out a spiritual life and a profession that would support us.

Eventually, with the support of my art professors from CSU Sacramento and UC Davis I went on to study for an MFA in the midwest. However, I do not want to romanticize those years. I was very young and inexperienced to be a parent to my kids, and I did not always choose what was good for them. They are shaped by the Movement experience, it is as much an integral part of their upbringing as it is mine. And because I have grown up with children, the work I do has always been cyclical—in those days making art was in the heart of our living room studio, now I make art in a studio in the middle of UCSB campus, integrated with my teaching practice and community projects.

Maya: How have you seen the art world change throughout your career?

Celia: I am still waiting to see true structural change. Tell me what has changed in the art world? It continues to be a eurocentric exclusive structure. Every so often they select a person who can get through the door. They select a person who most closely challenges them, but resembles them - someone who is in conversation with their linear perspective.

Cherríe: She is talking about the one person of color.

Maya: It's perpetuating that same paradigm, because they are all in response to the canon.

Celia: They (the artist of color) could be doing something culturally different, but it has to reflect the eurocentric world.

Cherríe: Even if it is a Fuck You to the eurocentric world.

Maya: It's still a counterpoint.

Celia: They are the pepper in the salt shaker—you definitely see them. For the most part it's men, for the most part, it's white men. For the most part, it's old white men and young white men. That's what I have seen over the last 40+ years and it has not changed very much. Yes, women come in to the work, and their work is celebrated. But, and I hate to be cynical, when I see the real elements of making art, the kind of support an artist needs - the financial support, the emotional and spiritual support, the intellectual support, the documentation, collection, interpretation, things that museums and art institutions are supposed to do in community - the sales of the work, the valuing of the work, the validation of the work - I haven't seen that change since I have been working - over the last 40 years.

What I have seen, is that because of the internet, younger artists have managed to do what they want to do—they have managed to make space for themselves and to develop community for themselves and to do work in public independent of a lot of institutions. I find that really exciting. The internet allows for the independence of the artist; in some ways that's good. Whether it's sustainable, whether it manifests in the same way I was taught art should manifest itself—those are different questions. But, they are not really questions of the institution, other than how is the institution supporting these efforts? Mainstream arts institutions continue to be funded by government funds to some extent, and by investment from foundations - both private and public. So what are they supporting, *what initiatives are they creating to support new work by communities of color*?

I know I'm making a generalization based on my experience, but if you take a look at the art schools, arts programs in colleges and universities in California that are in the business of educating and training young artists. Schools that are actively trying to attract students of color into their programs, what do they have to offer young artists of color: Black, Latinx, Native students, other than the *one-size-fits-all eurocentric paradigm*? Are there courses in African and African American, Latinx, Chicana/o, Latin American, Native American, Indigenous Art Histories? Are there professors of color whose body, experience and practice reflects those students who have been traditionally un-represented in the development of curriculum and pedagogy of art practice? Without the scope of representation how does the structure change?

Maya: What is your process for remembering?

Celia: That's life's work. I feel like there is a memory that is bigger than me. There is my story and the stories I hear around me, and it was the stories I heard around me, that made me feel as if I was looking at a window into the future—but all I could see was what was contained within that window, knowing that there is something beyond the frame of the window. Re-Membering is making things visible, that are present but you have to develop the eyes to see.

Grounding myself has always been in remembering that I just have one little piece of the story. That I must work to visualize what's all around me, what's behind me, what's in front of me. The work of remembering requires an exploration of everything I can get my hands on—sitting and observing, dreaming, walking, reading. It's a process of experiencing things that appear or seem to be un-related, but are related. It's like meditation, allowing your mind to wander, unattached as scenes flash before you, not jumping to conclusions based on your assumptions but allowing things to connect. I think we Xicana/o Native Peoples know that our people/ancestors made ceremony of the practice of observation and in dialogue with their collective perception. This is then what I understand as an Indigenous Xicana *manda* for the making of art.

Maya: What are some of your artistic rituals?

Celia: Cleaning my studio—it really is. I clean, and I sweep and I arrange—I'm always creating the space itself.

The other part is allowing ideas to emerge. The ritual for me is allowing my materials and the concepts to connect and to show me what to do...it's not easy. My challenge is to stay focused, to pay attention without getting in my own way.

Maya: What are some of your tools for self preservation within institutions?

Celia: I find institutions dangerous and challenging. I see them in the purview of white men and everything they have constructed that I have had to get through to be at the same table. I believe in the strength of being on the outside, standing on my own ground. It is a position of power to be on the outside. However, at this time, I have accepted a teaching position at UC Santa Barbara which is closer to the center than I have ever been. For self-preservation I am relying on the common goals, experience and vision of folks, who see

themselves in service of the communities in which the institution is embedded.

Maya: What are your tools for self preservation & revolution?

Celia: That is hard to answer, because your question connects self preservation to revolution. The question is, whose revolution? I don't know that you make revolution alone and that you can think of 'self preservation', if you want to challenge the status quo. I have things in my head about *what revolution is supposed to look like*—so are we talking about a change in society or systematic structural change in our world? Sometimes I ask myself, do we just want a better America?... Do we just want better citizenship?... What does that mean? So then it comes back to self preservation—back to the same things such as how do I live? and how do I sustain myself within my work?

There are entire nations/people on this continent and around the world, just trying to survive and keep their children alive through war, environmental and economic disasters. Some years back I was reminded that we are the offspring of the five percent that survived the invasion and cultural genocide of the original peoples of this continent. Perhaps in our subconscious we still understand our great purpose is to stay alive, protect and raise our children—but, in our time, I would say the challenge is to stay alive in consciousness, as Cherríe says, to stay awake.

I think the story of La Llorona, as I understand it now, the pre-colonial version, was about finding and moving to safe ground in the midst of impending catastrophic changes. The de-colonial telling of La Llorona, is in responding to the impending catastrophe(s) of our times. Returning in our consciousness to the places of origin, the temples built on sacred sites, homeground that is not ordered by nation/state delineations but the considerations of our human relationships with all life in this planet. Perhaps we are the foundation stones of those that are coming. In Mexico, as the anthropologists start digging to unearth the temples, they find a temple, built over a temple, built over a temple—going all the way back thousands of years. We can see we go back a long time. Perhaps this is the foundational moment of a new direction in understanding our purpose as survivors, because there is no going back—we have to move forward; in a way that is going to assure we are part of the survival plan of this planet - that is the only thing I can think of when you ask me about survival / revolution.

Maya: Have you witnessed moments of this type of transformation in your work?

Celia: If I start from the origin of my work as "having purpose" then yes. I am responding to the fragmentation and scattering of my family, history and culture, and I've come to understand that I am part of the collective *us*, in re-assembling and reanimating what we imagine has been flung to the *four winds*. What does that work look like? It looks like what I am doing. So, the more I work, the more I know.

Maya: Who are some of the people or what fields have supported you and your work?

Celia: Communities and community organizations, that have engaged and sustained my work in Sacramento, San Francisco, Oakland and Chicago.

Cherríe Moraga who has invested in my work by inviting me to collaborate in the visualization of her words and worlds. Chicana/o Studies Program at U.C. Berkeley and Chicana and the Chicano Studies Department at U.C. Santa Barbara, that have engaged me to teach Chicana/o art history, theory and practice over the last 20 years. The San Francisco Arts Commission, private foundations and the City and County of San Francisco who have given me grants to make work. Art historians, scholars and curators such as Laura Perez, Constance Cortez, Maria Ester Fernandez, Dignidad Rebelde, Las Mujeres de Maíz, The CN Gorman Museum and my children and family. You ask me to make a list like this and I see that I am very blessed. I could name names and the list would go on and on.

Maya: How do you maintain the joy and fun in your art practice despite all of the challenges?

Celia: Well, Cherríe always said this to me, it is something that other artists have said to me, they repeat it to each other and I tend to forget it—because I tend to get upset and whine...I do. I was looking through my journals and I saw myself whining in 1998 and 2004 and 2007. Maybe whining is another one of those strategies, but the other one is - doing the work. Coming back to the work, because that is what really makes you not crazy.

Patio
Taller

Las Nieta
de Nonó

It had been put in my head that I had absolutely nothing. Even in that patio I felt disposed of everything that existed.

To submerge in the piles of memories and rubble that resided in the house for years, made the love it kept vibrate, against oblivion, those walls. And the inevitable question made itself more evident. What happens when the intimacy of a space transfigures?

The exhaustion of asking for permission and searching for papers, collecting signatures, obtaining authorization, sitting in the chair until it's your turn… forged a stronger desire to break the periphery of the gate with the street that connects it.

Se me había metido en la cabeza que no tenía nada de nada. Incluso en aquel patio sentía que estaba desposeída de todo cuanto existía.

Sumergirme entre el montón de recuerdos y escombros que residían en la casa por años, hizo vibrar el amor que guardaba, a fuerza de olvido, esas paredes. Y la pregunta inevitable se hizo más evidente. Qué pasa cuando la intimidad de un espacio se transfigura?

El cansancio de pedir permiso y buscar papeles, recopilar firmas, sacar sellos, sentarse en la silla hasta que toque el turno...hizo más fuerte el deseo de quebrar la periferia del portón con la calle que conecta.

Remedies / Remedios

1. Take the time to listen to each other

2. _____

3. Identificar, reconocer, cuidar y usar todos los recursos con los que cuenta nuestro barrio para sostener física y espiritualmente nuestra práctica

4. Center myself

5. Preparar remedios

6. Check my privilege

7. Be generous with my ancestors and my spirits

8. Go to art events

9. Meditate

10. Cazar iguanas

11. Freestyle

12. Fund people in my community

13. Spend time with nature

14. _____

15. Sembrar, cosechar e intercambiar frutos y medicinas de temporada

16. Collect, listen, make and share music

17. Cocinar recetas de mis abuelitas, amigas y tías

18. Be quiet and still

19. _____

20. Practice the impossible

21. Organize, cry and scream with each other

22. Compartir, intercambiar conocimiento con nuestra comunidad

23. Asegurar que nuestro arte sea accesible a toda la comunidad

24. Have intergenerational friendships

25. Laugh until I cry or cry until I laugh

26. Abrir nuestro patio y la casa de la familia como espacio de encuentro y
reunión para el barrio donde se generan vínculos que nos nutran a todes

27. Talk to my grandmother

28. Dialogar con mis Aires

29. In Xochitl In Cuicatl

30. _____

31. Build with sisters and search for sisters

32. Expandir nuestro espacio doméstico como una alternativa para presentar nuestro trabajo de manera que podamos prescindir de los modos de producción capitalista

33. Intentionality

34. _____

35. _____

36. _____

Biographies

<u>Nasim Aghili</u> is a director, writer and performer. Her performances, theatre installations and soundpieces always deal with the experience of existing and living in different forms of exile, this mainly through creating grievability and healing rituals. She is a member of the queer, feminist and post-colonial art group Ful, the collective behind anti-nationalistic cabaret Europa Europa, in collaboration with the pop duo The Knife and Manifiesto de las Madres in collaboration with the crossborder band Quiquiriquí Coyotas (Mexico/US) and Mexican musician Paulina Lasa. She also works in the art duo called aghili/karlsson, challenging institutions and the art system in Sweden and abroad, working with decolonizing strategies and methods for creating healing and strengthening the solidarity between oppressed groups beyond the traditional art scene. Nasim's works have been translated into different languages and performed in Mexico, U.S., Holland, Estonia, Belgium, Sápmi and Germany.
www.aghili-karlsson.se
www.manifiestodelasmadres.org
www.europaeuropa.se

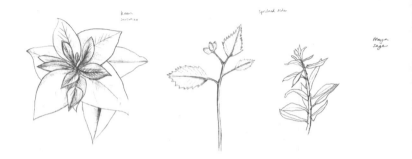

Onyinye Alheri is a visual artist born in Lagos, Nigeria & now newly based in Baltimore, MD after having called Oakland home for the last 5 years. Her work tests depths and boundaries of perception, drawing upon themes of ritual, illusion, formlessness and myth. She makes use of images & situations typically considered awkward and/or inconsequential so as to draw attention to the absurdities of mundane life and to the power that such phenomena have over how we connect with one another and our Selves. Alheri's work interrogates notions of culture, nationhood and identity at the collective level & in/visibility, madness, dualism, and ego at the individual level. At the core of her practice is a never-ending investigation into consciousness, which the artist seeks to deconstruct in order to celebrate the universal silence.

Vreni Michelini Castillo AKA Chhoti Maa is a multidisciplinary cultural producer with 11 years of experience; working through art, performance, cultural organizing, music, red medicine and traditional Mexican danza. Much of my work is rooted in Mexican oral tradition, specifically Grandma's storytelling magic. As part of the post-NAFTA diaspora, I was formed by my migrant experience. My work reflects decolonial living, contemporary Indigenous spirituality, queerness, migrant empowerment and the reconstruction of the womyn temple.

Jen Everett is an artist from Southfield, Michigan, currently working in Saint Louis, Missouri. Her recent work engages vernacular archives, the materials we collect, the records and information we hold in our bodies and where the two may converge. Her work has evolved from an image based practice to one incorporating texts, sculpture, installation and time based media. Jen's art making has been heavily influenced by her undergraduate training in architecture. Jen is currently a Chancellor's Graduate Fellow in the Sam Fox School of Design & Visual Arts at Washington University in Saint Louis. Jen's work has been shown at arts spaces including Leo Model Gallery at Hampshire College, Vox Populi in Philadelphia and Gallery 102 in Washington DC. Her work has also been published in Transition and SPOOK magazines. She has been an artist in residence at the Vermont Studio Center, Atlantic Center for the Arts and ACRE.

Maya Gomez is a California native. She received her Ed.M. concentrating on Arts in Education, from the Harvard Graduate School of Education and her B.A. in Art History and Dance from U.C. Santa Barbara. Maya spent the last 10 years working with youth in the Mission District of San Francisco. A few months ago, she moved to Santa Barbara where she spends her days cooking, reading and writing.

Keara Gray was born and raised in San Francisco CA. I'm 17 years old and a senior attending Phillip Sala Burton High School. Some hobbies that I love to do are play sports, hike, read, and make art. I've always written poems and songs since I was young; my inspiration stems from my family members. I started exploring mediums beyond poetry when I began an internship at Southern Exposure. Now I work with paint, sculpture, and sound. My work has been shown at Southern Exposure and Root Division.

Shylah Pacheco Hamilton is an Afrosurrealist filmmaker whose creative research interests meet at the crossroads of experimental video, Black and Chicana feminist theory, and ritual performance. Her most recent work consists of experimental video and installations that explore social justice, memory, dreams, and ritual performances of the sacred. Selected exhibitions include The Hague, Dok Leipzig, Cine-Palium Fest, DMZ International Documentary Film Festival, L'Alternativa, It's All True International Documentary Film Festival, SFMOMA, SomArts, Oakland Underground Film Festival, International Black Women's Film Festival, and The San Francisco Black Film Festival. Her work was also featured in the Rush Philanthropic Arts Foundation's *Power, Protest & Resistance: The Art of Revolution* exhibition in NYC. Shylah lives in Oakland and is a member of the artist collective, The Black Woman Is God. Her writings can be found in Ana Castillo's *La Tolteca Magazine*, *Voices of the Ancestors Calling* (forthcoming anthology, Demeter Press) and *Iyanifa Woman of Wisdom: Insights from the Priestesses of the Ifa Orisha Tradition, Their Stories*, and *Plight for the Divine Feminine*.

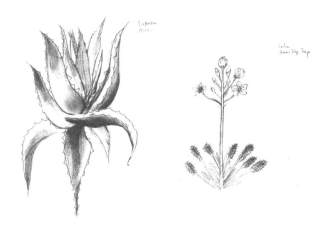

Shah Noor Hussein is a writer and educator with an M.A. in Anthropology focusing on black feminism, diaspora studies and liberatory pedagogies. Shah has served as editor and publisher of two poetry anthologies, a magazine and a book. They have been published in *Nook & Kranny*, *The Black Aesthetic*, *CUNJUH*, *Mancha Mag*, *Veudux Child* and *Umber* magazine. Shah has earned national and international funding opportunities to support their creative career work, including the Hollings, Udall, Boren and Davis-Putter awards as well as the CWS Curriculum Development Grant, SWS Diversity & Mentorship Grant and the STEM Grant for Higher Education. From 2015 to 2017, Shah served as Writing & Scholarship Fellow at the California Institute of Integral Studies developing curriculums, producing writing workshops, teaching courses, and working with students from diverse backgrounds on creative and academic material. They are currently a Guest Lecturer in the Bay Area Community College System as well as a freelance writer and editor.

During the 2018 - 2019 school year, Shah will be a Diversity Teaching Fellow for the Peralta District Community Colleges while working on two forthcoming publications and toward their PhD in Anthropology.

Melinda Luisa de Jesús is Associate Professor and former Chair of Diversity Studies at California College of the Arts. She writes and teaches about Filipinx/American cultural production, girl culture, monsters, and race/ethnicity in the United States. She edited *Pinay Power: Peminist Critical Theory*, the first anthology of Filipina/American feminisms (Routledge 2005). Her writing has appeared in *Mothering in East Asian Communities: Politics and Practices*; *Completely Mixed Up: Mixed Heritage Asian North American Writing and Art*; *Approaches to Teaching Multicultural Comics*; *Ethnic Literary Traditions in Children's Literature*; *Challenging Homophobia*; *Radical Teacher*; *The Lion and the Unicorn; Ano Ba Magazine*; *Rigorous*; *Konch Magazine*; *Rabbit and Rose*; *MELUS*; *Meridians*; *The Journal of Asian American*

Studies, and *Delinquents and Debutantes: Twentieth-Century American Girls' Cultures*.

She is also a poet and her chapbooks, *Humpty Drumpfty and Other Poems*, *Petty Poetry for SCROTUS Girls' with poems for Elizabeth Warren and Michelle Obama*, *Defying Trumplandia*, *Adios Trumplandia*, *James Brown's Wig and Other Poems*, and *Vagenda of Manicide and Other Poems* were published by Locofo Chaps in 2017. Her first collection of poetry, *peminology*, was recently published by Paloma Press (March 2018). She is a mezzo-soprano, a mom, an Aquarian, and admits an obsession with Hello Kitty. More info: *http://peminist.com*

The sisters Lydela (1979) and Michel (1982) are <u>Las Nietas de Nonó</u>. They live in Barrio San Antón, a half rural, half industrial working class neighborhood of Carolina, Puerto Rico. Their autobiographical work is framed within the socio-economic and geographical context of the exclusion and eviction of black communities in Puerto Rico, which includes racial and class discrimination, mass incarceration, drug trafficking, obstetric violence, and the cycle of poverty. Their practice also highlights circumstances and elements that are present in their neighborhood: the expansion of ancestral knowledge, the exchange of produce grown in the neighborhood, and the re-use of materials found in the area to create artistic projects. Las Nietas de Nonó play within the intersection of theater, performance, dance, visual art, activism, ecology and emancipatory education. They created *Patio Taller* in what used to be their paternal grandparents home. This space is a house, but it is also a community art

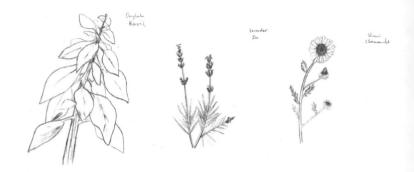

space, a garden, and it is used for public gatherings, performance, international artist residencies, workshops, sustainable agriculture and cooking. Their work has been presented in Puerto Rico, Dominican Republic, Haiti, Cuba, United States, England and has being comisionado by the X Berlin Biennale. Las Nietas de Nonó received the United State Artist Fellowship, the Art Of Change Award from Ford Foundation and the Global Art Fund from Astraea.

Grace Rosario Perkins (b. 1986, Santa Fe, NM) is an Albuquerque and Bay Area-based artist who has spent most of her life living between city centers, as well the Navajo Nation, and the Gila River Indian Community. Her work examines cultural dissonance, disassembling and rebuilding personal history through explorations with color, abstraction, and language. Perkins' practice, which includes painting, printmaking, sculpture, and performance, is highly collaborative and often made with family members such as her father Olen Perkins, and artists from her indigenous and DIY communities. She was a founding member of Black Salt Collective, a group of women artists of color that worked to amplify black and indigenous voices through curatorial projects, publications, and performance. Perkins has lectured at venues such as Mills College, Pomona College, UC Santa Barbara, Occidental College, the San Francisco Public Library, Real Time and Space Oakland, and the Museum of Arts and Design, New York. She has been an artist in residence at Facebook HQ, ACRE, Varda Artists Residency, Sedona Summer Colony, White Leaves, Kala Art Institute, and was nominated for the Liquitex Painter's Residency, SFMOMA SECA Award, and Tosa Studio Award at Minnesota Street Project.

Celia Herrera Rodríguez (Xicana/O'dami) is a painter, performance and installation artist whose work reflects a full generation of dialogue with Chicano, Native American, Pre-Columbian, and Mexican thought. Originally from Sacramento, Herrera received her B.A. in Art & Ethnic Studies from CSU-Sacramento and a M.F.A. in Painting from the University of Illinois, Urbana-Champaign. She has held appointments at Stanford University, UC Santa Cruz, the School of the Art Institute of Chicago, UC Berkeley, and California College of the Arts. Her paintings, drawings and installation work have been exhibited nationally, including: The Triton Museum, Santa Clara; Glass Curtain Gallery at Columbia College of Chicago; CN Gorman Museum, UC-Davis; The DeSaisset Museum at Santa Clara University; The Institute of American Indian Art Museum in Santa Fe; The Oakland Museum of California; Tufts University Gallery (Medford, MA); The Mexican Museum of San Francisco; C.A.G.E. Gallery (Cincinnati); and, Name Gallery (Chicago). She has also shown Internationally at the University of Cork (Ireland), The Centro Cultural Santo Domingo (Oaxaca, México), the Centro Colombo Americano (Medellin, Colombia) among others. Her work is permanently housed in a number of private and public collections, including the Mexican Fine Arts Center Museum in Chicago, and the Institute of American Indian Art Museum of Santa Fe. Since the mid-90s, Herrera has performed with many of her installations as stagings. In her performances, the cultural symbology of her paintings moves into the three-dimensional world of MeXicana and Indigenous history. In recent years, she has applied her vision as a conceptual artist to set and costume design, chiefly in collaboration with playwright, Cherríe Moraga. Herrera's design work includes: "The Hungry Woman" (Stanford University); "La Semilla Caminante" (Intersection for the Arts, SF); "Digging Up the Dirt" (Breath of Fire Theater, Santa Ana); and "New Fire, To Put Things Right Again" (Brava Theater, SF). In 2011, a series of her line drawings were also published in Moraga's collection of essays: "Xicana Codex of Changing Consciousness, Writing 2000- 2010," published by Duke University Press. Herrera recently moved to Santa Barbara where she co-directs Las Maestras Center for Xicana Indigenous Thought and Art Practice and teaches Contemporary Chicano Art at UC Santa Barbara.

Lukaza Branfman-Verissimo received her BFA from California College of the Arts. She has had solo exhibitions at Deli Gallery in Long Island City, NY, Lago Projects in Oakland, E.M. Wolfman in Oakland, and Bolivar Gallery in Los An-

geles. Her work has been included in exhibitions and performances at Betti Ono Gallery, Root Division, Deli Gallery, Southern Exposure, SFMOMA, Kala Art Institute, Osaka Art University, the Berkeley Art Museum and Pacific Film Archive and Highways Performance Space. Lukaza was a Yozo Hamaguchi fellow at Kala Art institute in 2015 and has been a visiting artist at the College of Design, Architecture, Art Practice at University of Cincinnati, at New York University, at California College of the Arts and at Mills College. She is the co-founder and lead curator at Nook Gallery, a member of CTRL+SHFT Collective and the Visual Arts Editor for *New Life Quarterly* Magazine.

Leila Weefur lives and works in Oakland, CA. Weefur received her MFA from Mills College and her BFA from CSU Los Angeles, and Howard University. With a multidisciplinary practice, Weefur tackles the complexities of phenomenological Blackness through video, installation, printmaking, and lecture-performances. Using materials and visual gestures to access the tactile memory, she explores the abject, the sensual and the nuance found in the social interactions and language with which our bodies have to negotiate space. She is a recipient of the Hung Liu award, the Murphy & Cadogan award, and the Walter & Elise Haas Creative Work Fund. Weefur has exhibited her work in local and national galleries including Southern Exposure and SOMArts Gallery in San Francisco, Betti Ono in Oakland, BAMPFA and Smack Mellon in Brooklyn, New York. She is the Audio/Video, Editor In Chief at Art Practical and member of The Black Aesthetic.

Acknowledgments

Grateful acknowledgment is made to everyone at Wolfman Books and Small Press, especially Justin Carder for serving as a catalyst and confidant for this collection of reflections.

Gratitude to the artists for their commitment to working in the arts, Keara Gray, Jen Everett, Grace Rosario Perkins, Melinda Luisa de Jesús, Shylah Pacheco Hamilton, Leila Weefur, Onyinye Alheri, Shah Noor Hussein, Nasim Aghili, Las Nietas de Nonó, Lukaza Branfman-Verissimo.

To Jeff Valenzuela for connecting us to the Caravana, for documenting our ceremonies and guiding us through Tijuana.

To Celia Herrera Rodríguez and Cherríe Moraga for their guidance and wisdom, for bringing us together for Un Llanto Colectivo and continuing to forge pathways through Las Maestras Center for Xicana Indigenous Thought & Art Practice.

Agradecidas con la Tierra, con las energías, con el aquí y el ahora. Siguiendo el camino de nuestres pueblos y ancestres. Abriendo campo pa' las próximas 7 generaciones.

Selected Bibliography

Ahmed, Sara. *On being included: Racism and diversity in institutional life.* Duke University Press, 2012.

Anzaldúa, Gloria. *Borderlands: la frontera. Vol. 3.* San Francisco: Aunt Lute, 1987.

Anzaldúa, Gloria. *Light in the dark/Luz en lo oscuro: Rewriting identity, spirituality, reality.* Duke University Press, 2015.

Batchelor, David. *Chromophobia.* Reaktion books, 2000.

Benedetti, Maria. *Sembrando y Sanando en Puerto Rico.* Verde Luz. 1996.

Bruguera, Tania. *www.arte-util.org*

Cha, Theresa Hak Kyung. *Dictee.* Univ of California Press, 2001.

Chang, Jeff. *We gon'be alright: Notes on race and resegregation.* Macmillan, 2016.

Crenshaw, Kimberlé. *On Intersectionality: Essential Writings.* The New Press, 2019.

Cuevas, Minerva. *Antithesis 2 Donald McRonald.* Alias 2012.

Davis, Angela Y. *Women, race, & class.* Vintage, 2011.

Ewen, Stuart, and Elizabeth Ewen. *Typecasting: On the arts and sciences of human inequality.* Seven Stories Press, 2011.

Ex-Workers' Collective, CrimethInc. *Expect Resistance: a field manual.* 2008.

Freire, Paulo. *Pedagogy of the oppressed.* Bloomsbury Publishing USA, 2018.

Gonzales, Patrisia. *Red medicine: Traditional Indigenous rites of birthing and healing.* University of Arizona Press, 2012.

Gonzales Perez, Karolina. *Nawi.* 2018

Hooks, Bell. "Art on my mind: Visual politics." (1996).

Isaacson, Johanna. "From Riot Grrrl to CrimethInc: A Lineage of Expressive Negation in Feminist Punk and Queercore." *Liminalities: A Journal of Performance Studies* 7.4, pg. 1-18. 2011.

La Pocha Nostra. *Manifesto for a Post Democratic Era.* Gato Negro, 2018

Lorde, Audre. *Sister outsider: Essays and speeches.* Crossing Press, 2012.

Moraga, Cherríe, and Gloria Anzaldúa, eds. *This bridge called my back: Writings by radical women of color.* Suny Press, 2015.

Rankine, Claudia. *Citizen: an American lyric.* Graywolf Press, 2014.

Riggs, Marlon. *Tongues Untied.* 1989.

Román, Estela. *Nuestra Medicina: de los Remedios para el Aire y los Remedios para el Alma.* Palibrio, 2012.

LIGHT PINK

GRE

BLACK

JOYCE SCOTT

KEARA

ANGELA DAVIS

AVA DUVERNAY

ORAN

YELLOW

YELLOW

MY GREAT-AUNT
YETTA STROMBERG

ANGELA DAVIS

GRACE LEE BOGGS

LUKAZA   RICK LOWE

MY MOTHER SUCHI BRANFMAN

INDIRA ALLEGR

ASUKA HISA
AUDRE LORDE   JAMILLAH JAMES

NOAH PURIFOY

ORANGE

HOLLEY

PAUL RIEGE MY GRANDMOTHER HELEN MCCABE

GRACE MY GREAT-GRANDMOTHER NELLIE NATONAB

POLY STYRENE JAUNE QUICK-TO-SEE-SMITH

RED EARTH TONES

OCHRE

TINA CAMPT

DIONNE BRAND

SAIDIYA HARTMAN JENN AN

TONI MORRISON

CARRIE MAE WEEMS

ZORA NEAL HURSTON SADE

MARY LOU WILLIAMS

BLACK BLUE

WESTIN TERUYA

ADEE ROBERSON LEILA MAYSOUN WAZWAZ

MICHELE CARLSON

ESSENCE HARDEN

PURPLE ANYTHIN

DARK

INDIGO BLUE

MAXINE HONG KINGSTON
LENY STROBEL
PINK MELINDA
EVELINA GALAN
VIRGINA CERENIO
JANICE SAPIGO TRINIDAD E
CELIA H. RODRIGUEZ DR. DAWN MA
A BAKER CHERRIE MORAGA
GLORIA ANZALDUA
GOLD

FRANK LA PINA CHERRIE MORAGA
CRAFT: EMBROIDERY, THREA
WEAVING, GLYPHS, PETRO
JOSE MONTOYA CELIA PICTOGRAMS, STORY STO
ESTEBAN VILLA NATURE GLORIA AN
FAIRY TALES

WINNIE MANDELA
IYANIE
ANA CAST
KORRYN GAINES
SAN

A

GREEN

GLORIA ANZALDUA

SARAH LAWRENCE LIGHTFOOT

ANGELA DAVIS

BLAC

RED **MAYA** DOLORES HUERTA

BELL HOOKS

MAMA HELENA VIRAMONTES

MAYA ANGELOU DORA CHAVEZ

MY GRANDMOTHER

PURPLE BLACK

TO

LAVENDER

KS, BABY ARISIKA RAZAK

BLUE BELL HOOKS BE

ALICE WALKER **SHAH**

AH ZORA NEAL HURSTON

ISAH REISH AUDRE LORDE

CELI.

JAQUI ALEXANDER GOLDEN

BLAND YELLOW

INE PURPLE REEN

ABI JUANITA　　　　PUSHPAMALA

V. SHAHMUSH PARSIPUA

ANCESTOR CAMILA　　　NALINI

ROBIN BERNSTEIN　　　GLORIA ANZALDUA

VANIA MICHELINI CASTILLO

CK LADZEKPO　　HOPE GINSBURG

LUIS BARRAGAN　　　ANATA ISOZAKI

ALLAN DESOUZA　　　　　　TURQ

DUBOVSKY & CHICVEYI COATL　　PASTOR VEGA

THERESA HAK KYUNG CHA

MINERVA CUEVAS　　　　　DAUGHTERS

TANIA BRUGUERA

FRANCIS ALYS　　ESTELA ROMAN

REGINA JOSE GALINDO　　　　ALL S

WILLIAM POPE L.

SHIRIN NESHAT

PATRISIA GONZALES

TEHCHING HSIEH　　　EDGAR CAYCE

RUZ　　　GUILLERMO GOMEZ PEÑA

ISABEL ALLENDE　　　BUENA VISTA SOCIAL CLUB

MICHAEL JACKSON　　ERYKAH BADU　　DA

CHAVELA VARGAS　　　MALA RODRIGUEZ

QUINCY JONES　　　　　MARE A

BEING A PART

OF STANDING ROCK

RED CLAY

BEESWAX YELLOW